FRANZ LISZT

Rhapsodies Hongroises

For the Piano

Edited by

RAFAEL JOSEFFY

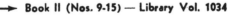

IN TWO BOOKS

Book I (Nos. 1- 8) — Library Vol. 1033

→ Book II (Nos. 9-15) — Library Vol. 1034

G. SCHIRMER, Inc.

DISTRIBUTED BY

HAL•LEONARD® CORPORATION

7777 W. BLUEMOUND RD. P.O. BOX 13819 MILWAUKEE, WI 53213

A H. W. Ernst

Rhapsodie hongroise Nº 9
Le Carnaval de Pesth

Edited and revised by
Rafael Joseffy

Fr. Liszt

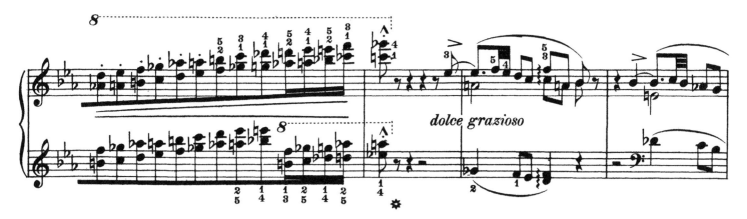

25312 c

Newly-revised Edition

Printed in the U. S. A.

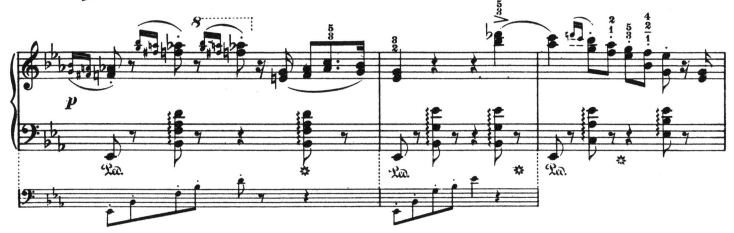

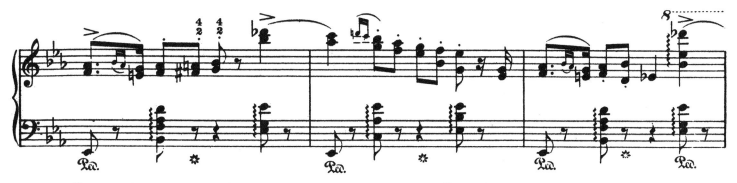

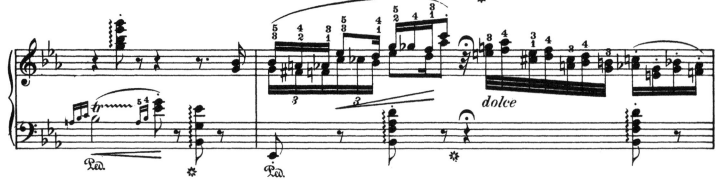

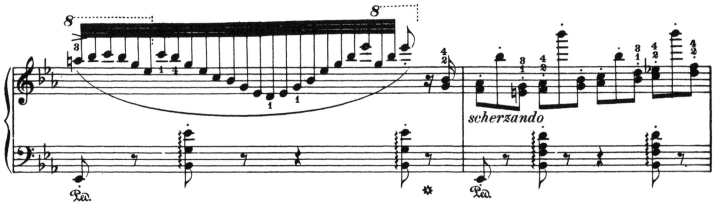

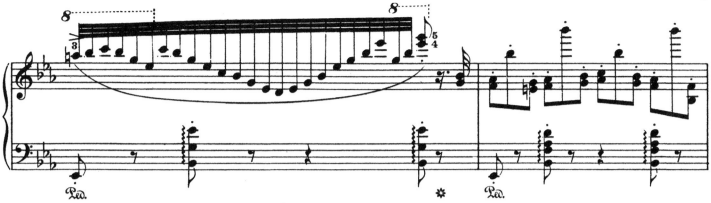

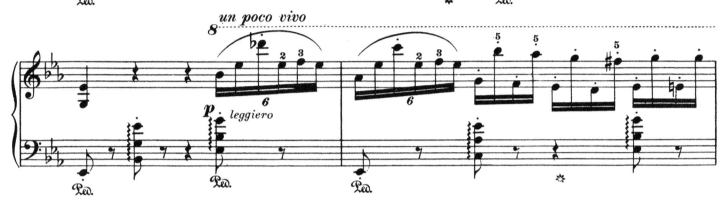

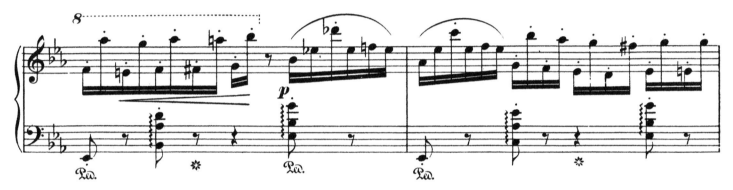

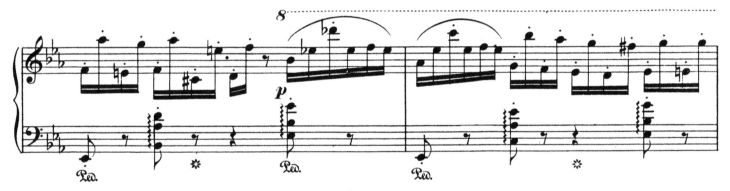

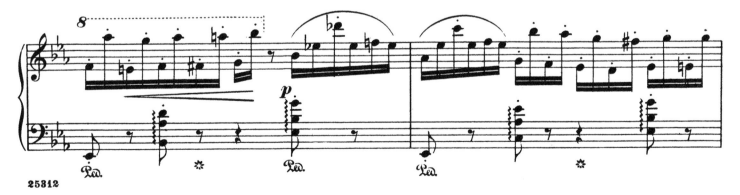

8

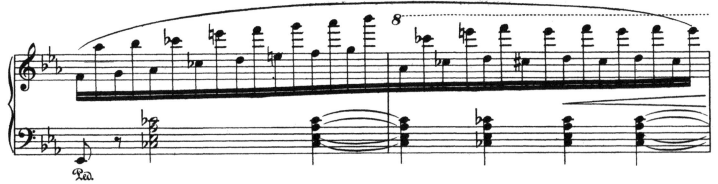

Piano à 6 Oct.

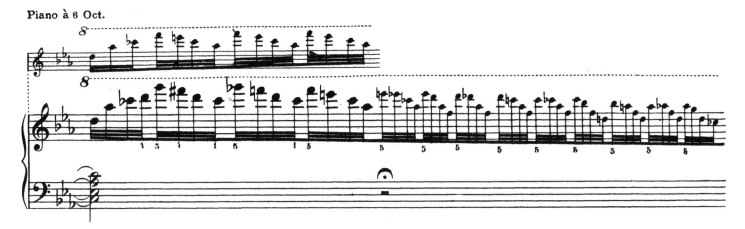

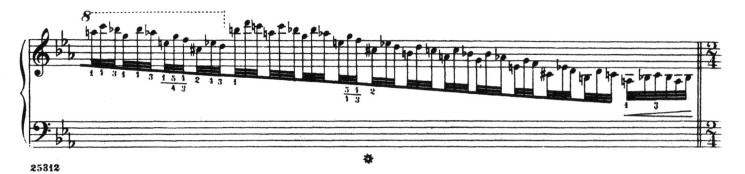

25312

Allegretto

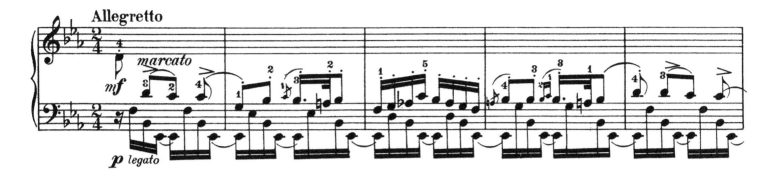

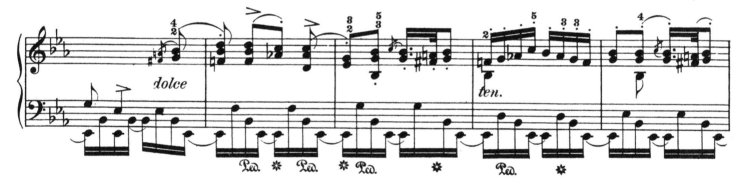

25312

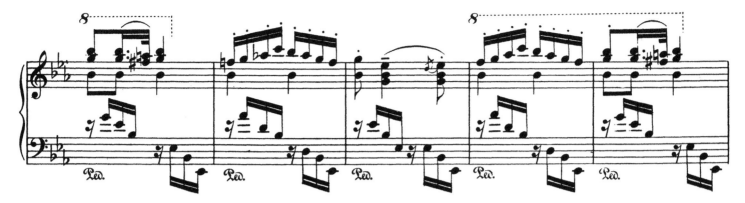

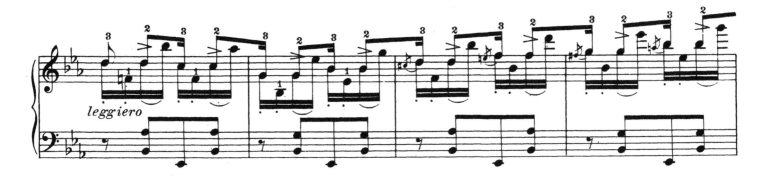

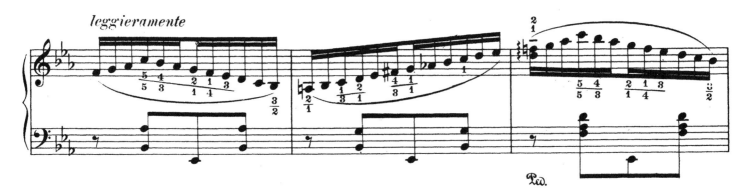

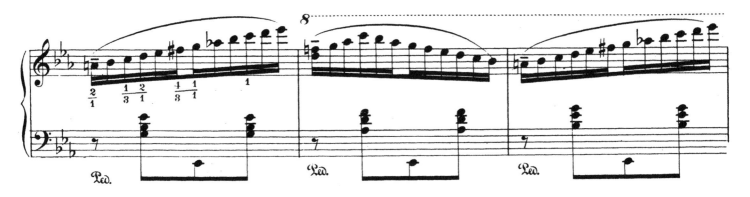

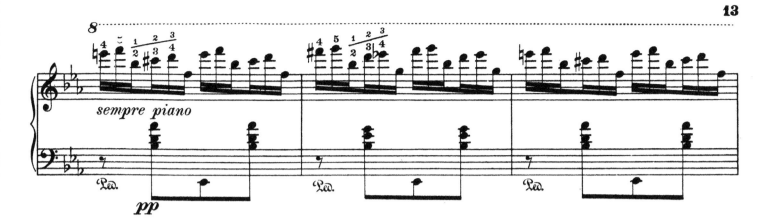

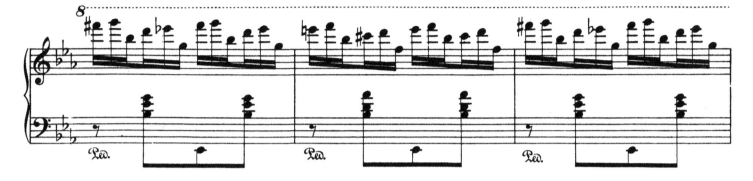

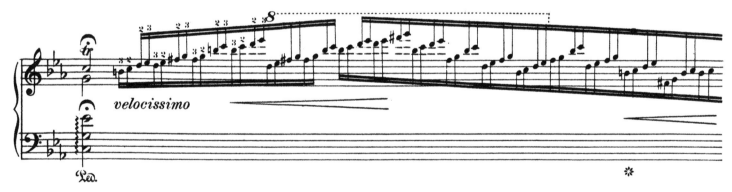

25312

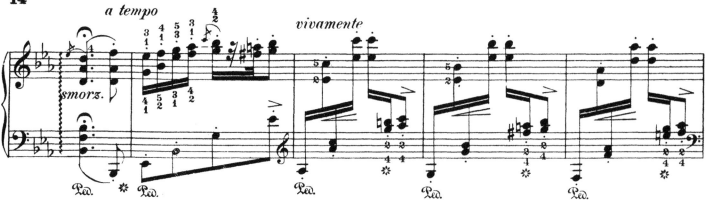

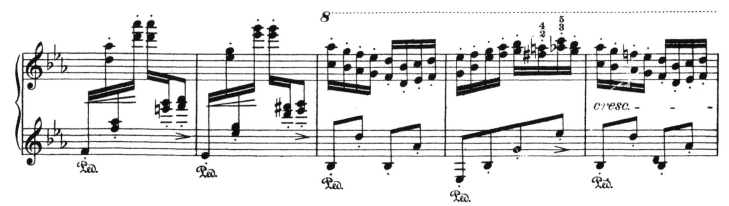

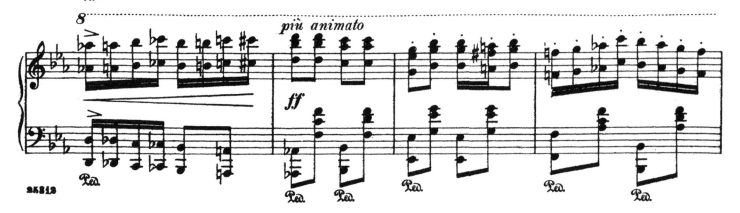

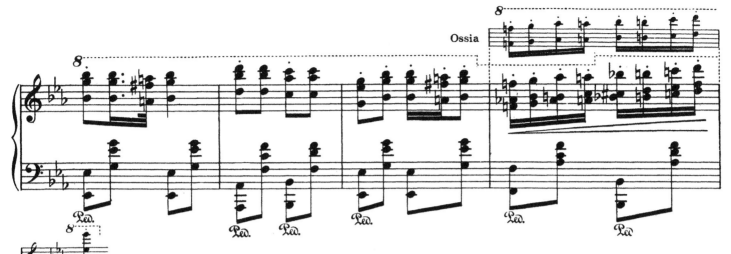

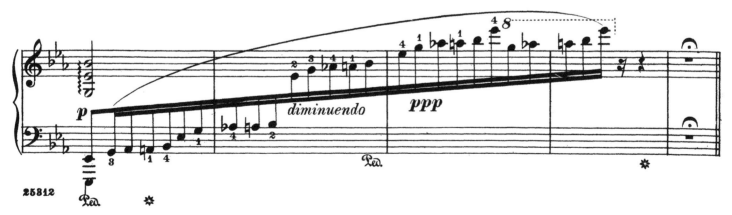

Finale

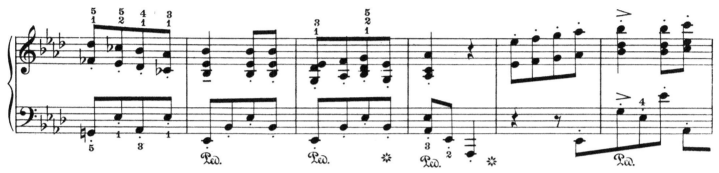

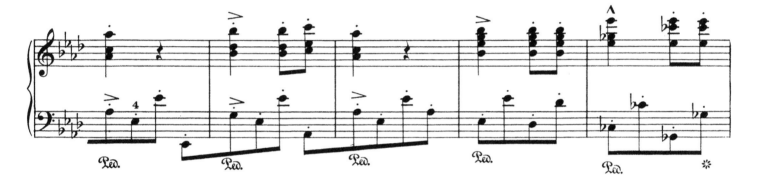

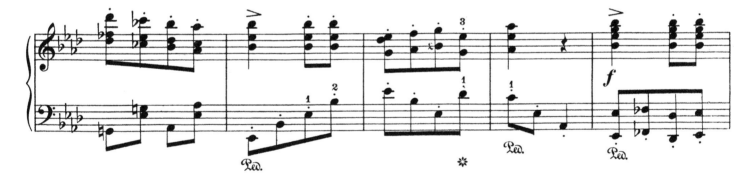

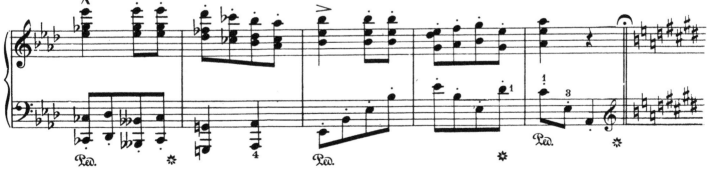

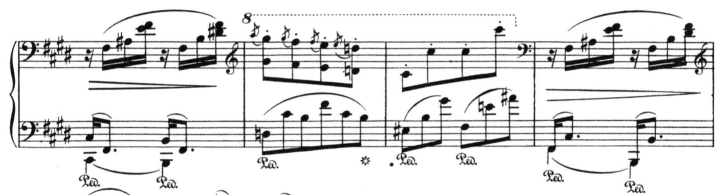

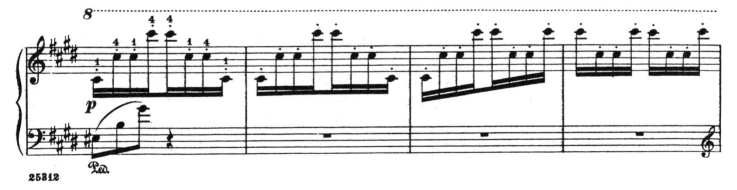

25312

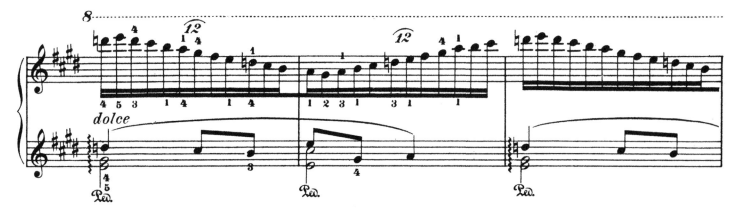

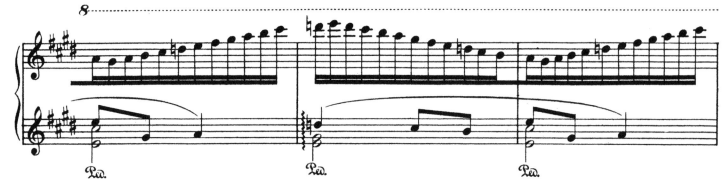

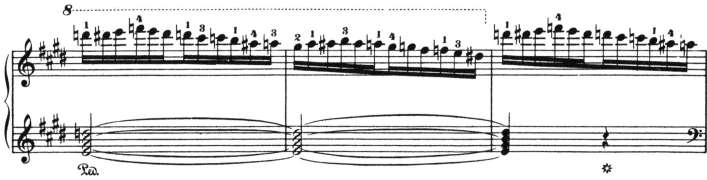

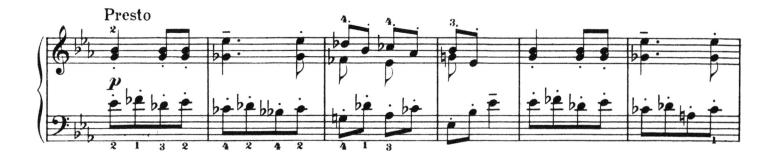

Più animato

fff tumultuoso

8va bassa

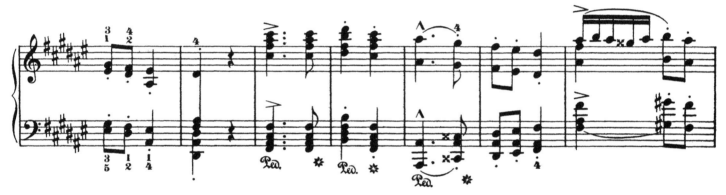

sempre fff

8va bassa

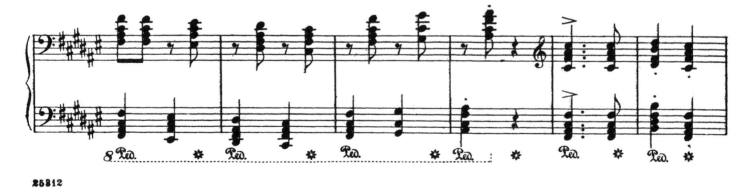

25312

Allegro moderato

ff *e marcatissimo il tema*

poco rall.

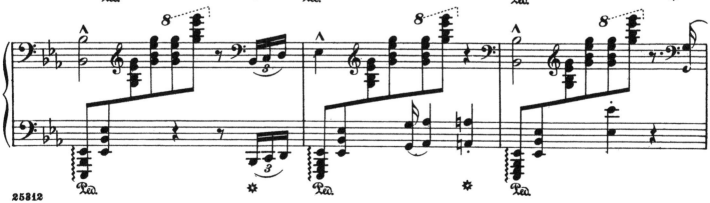

incalzando e stringendo fine al Presto

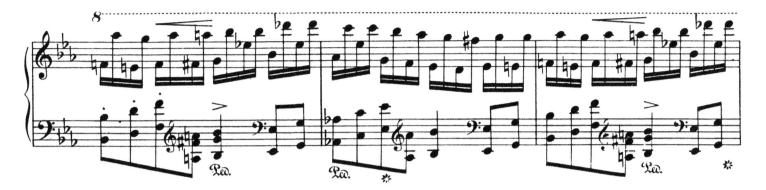

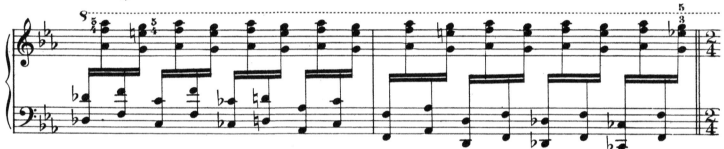

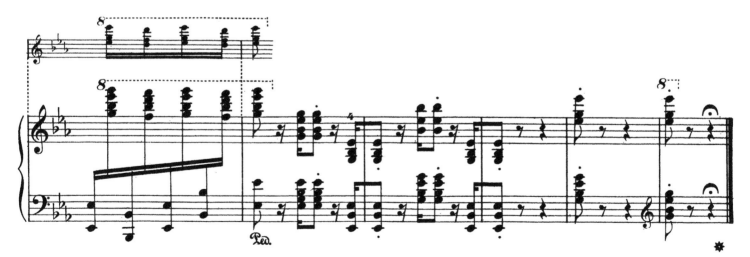

25812

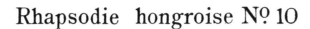

À Egressy Bény

Rhapsodie hongroise № 10

Edited and revised by
Rafael Joseffy

Fr. Liszt

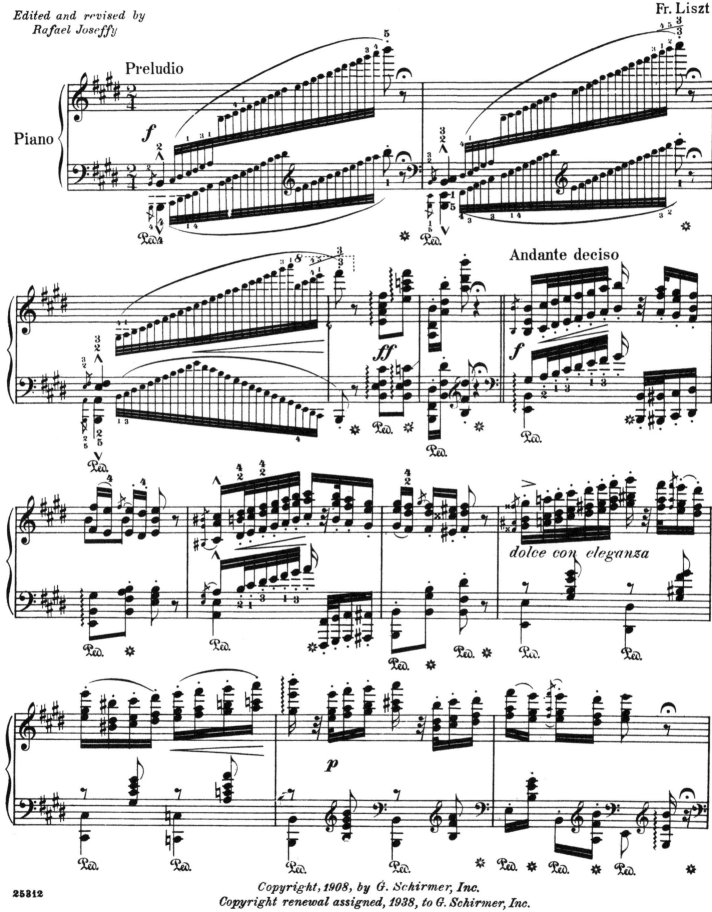

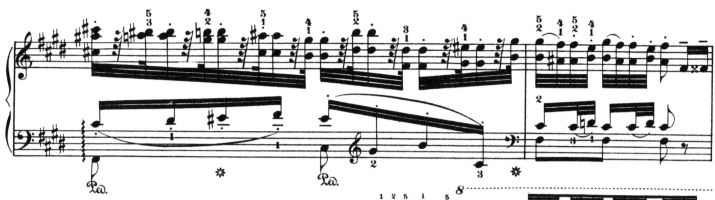

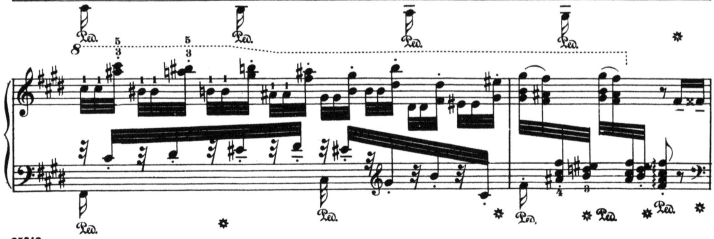

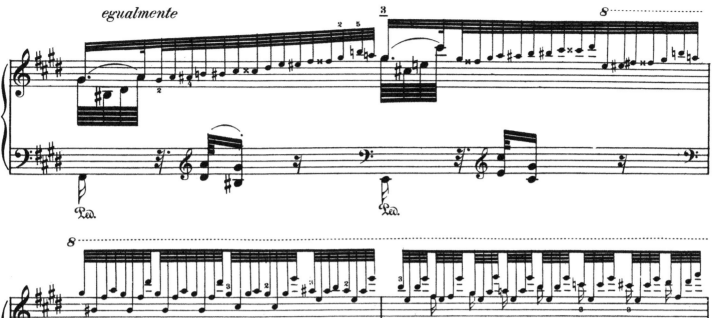

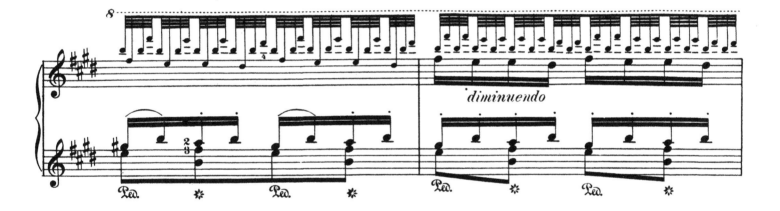

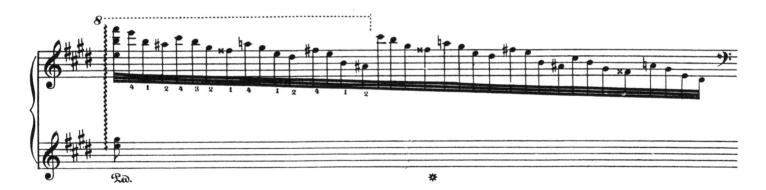

25312

Allegretto capriccioso

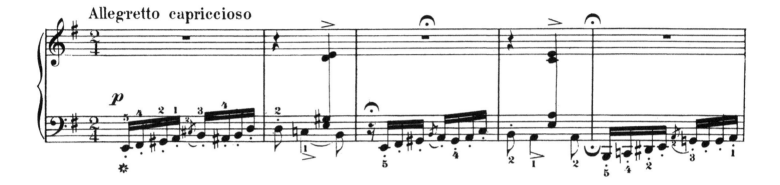

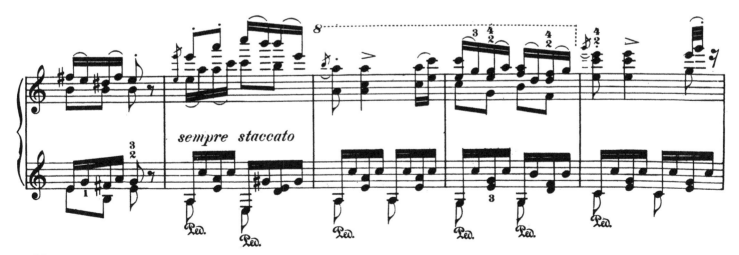

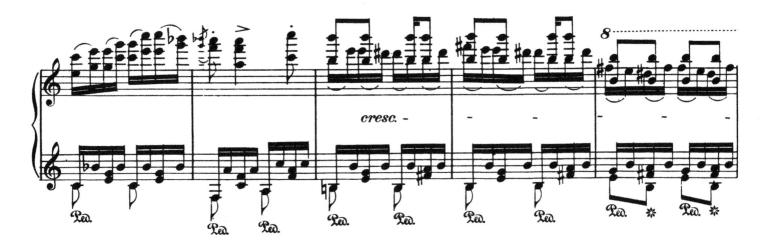

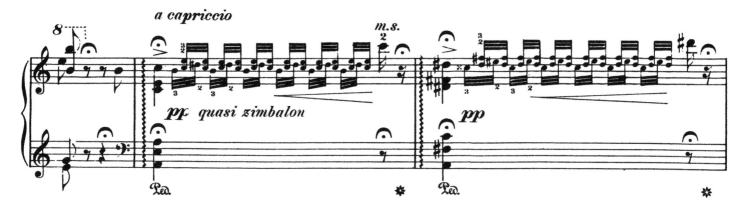

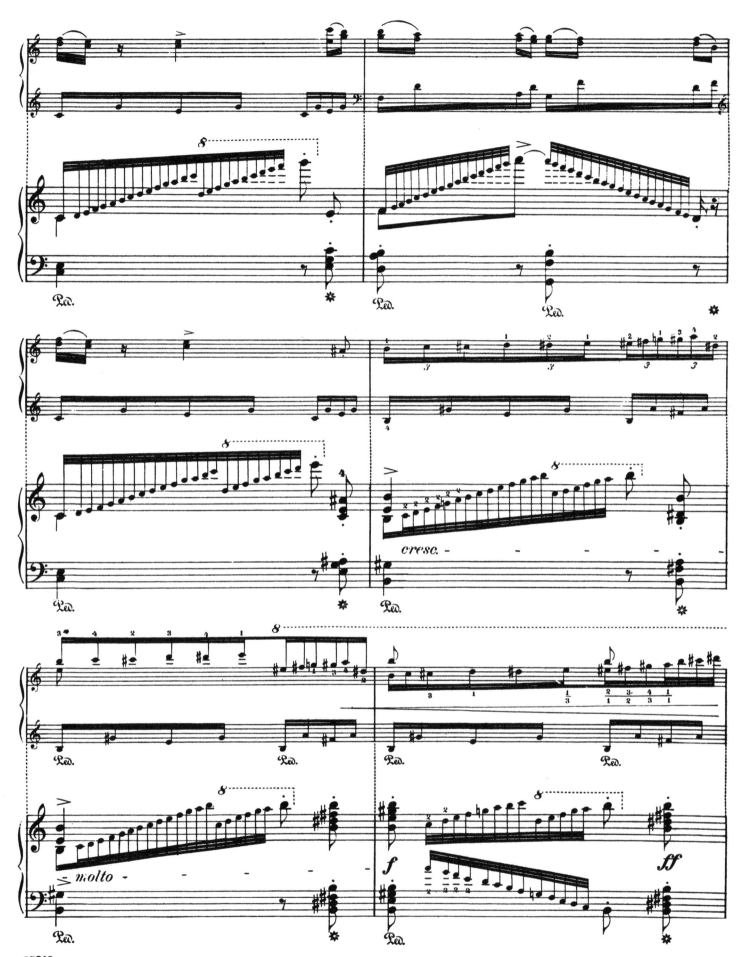

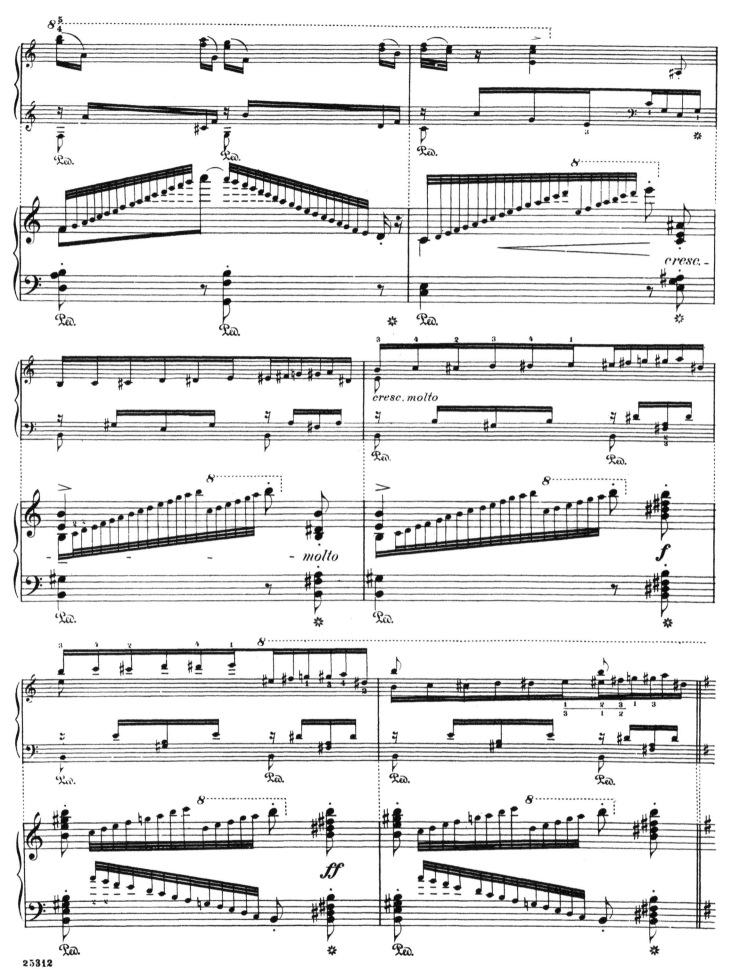

Più animato

sempre forte brioso

stringendo

Vivacissimo giocoso assai

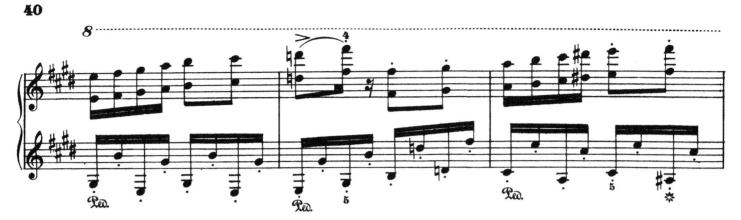

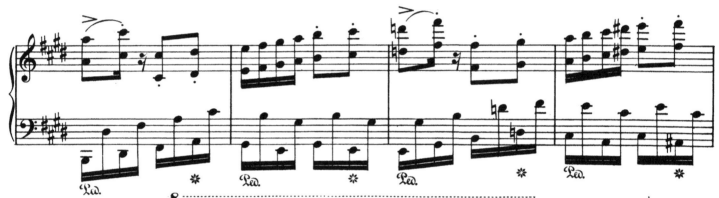

Au Baron Fery Orczy

Rhapsodie hongroise № 11

Edited and revised by
Rafael Joseffy

Fr. Liszt

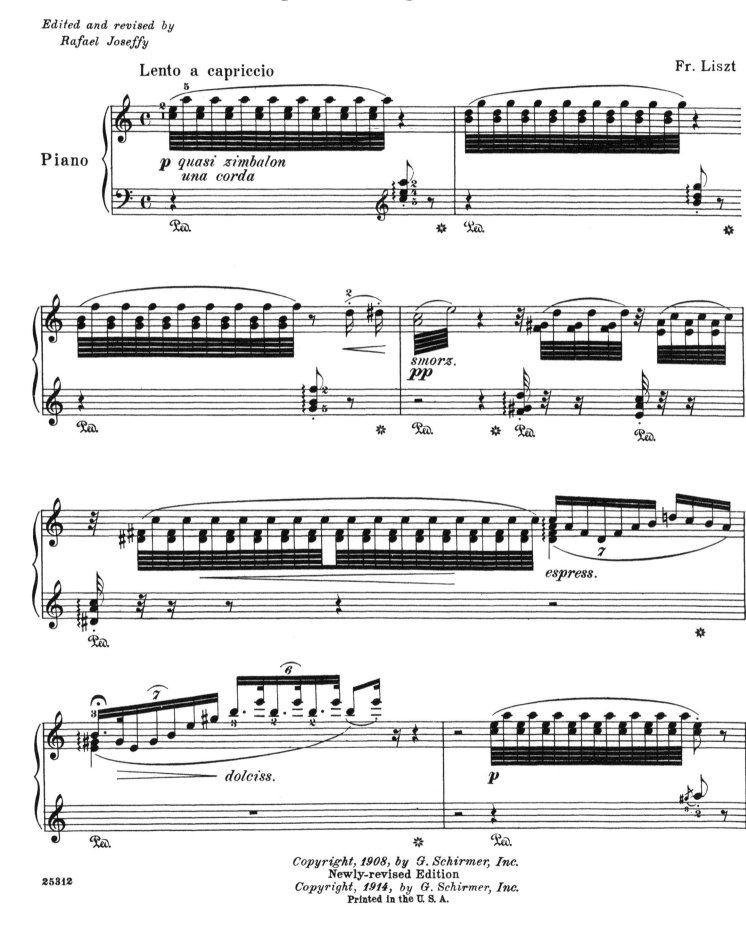

25312

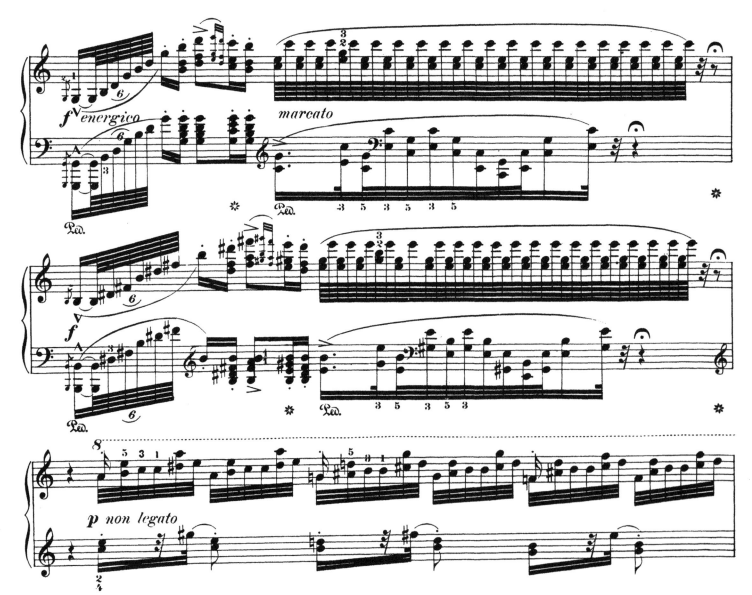

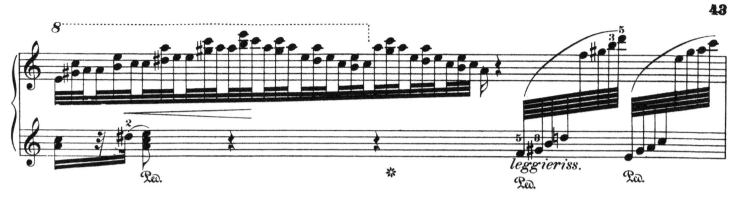

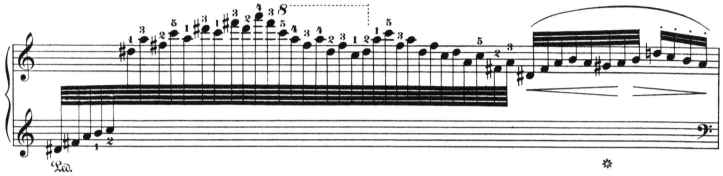

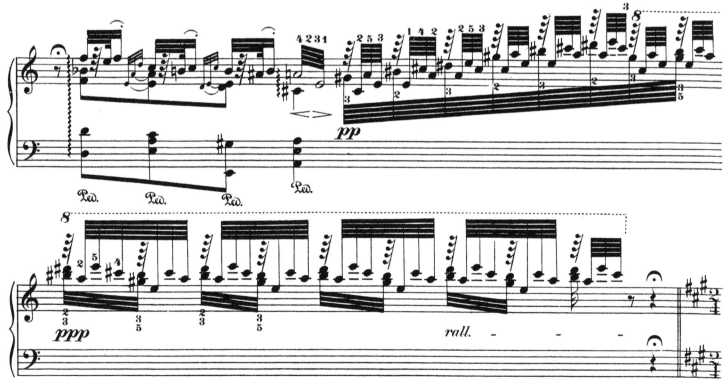

Andante sostenuto

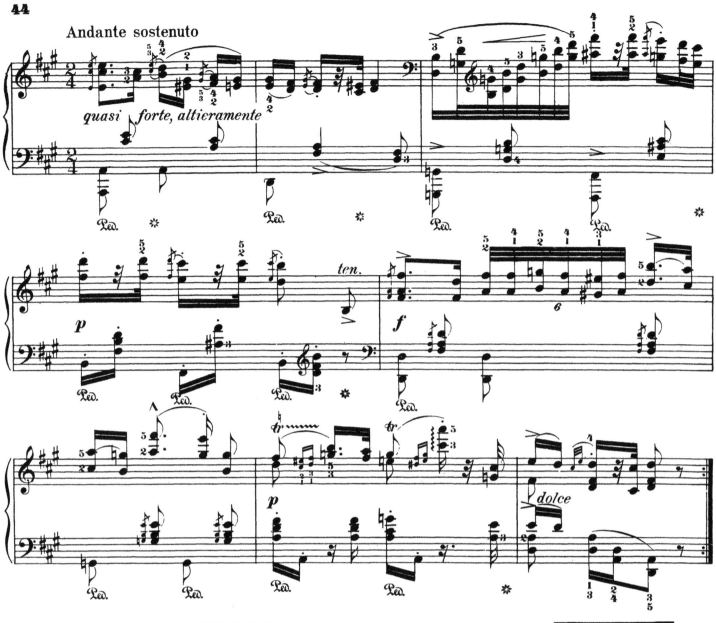

quasi forte, alteramente

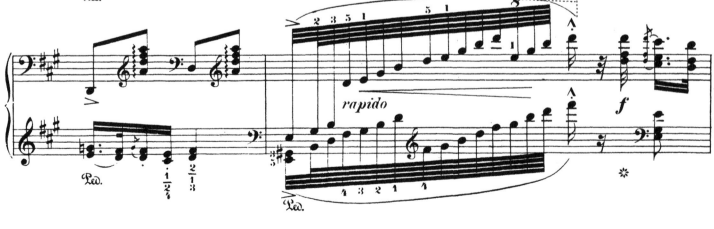

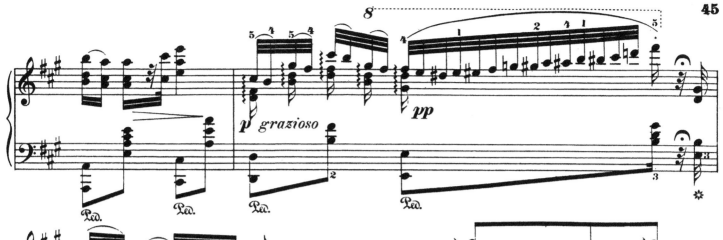

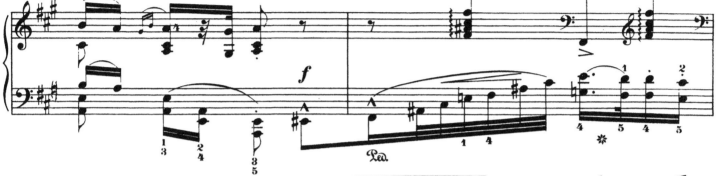

Vivace assai

dim.

25312

25312

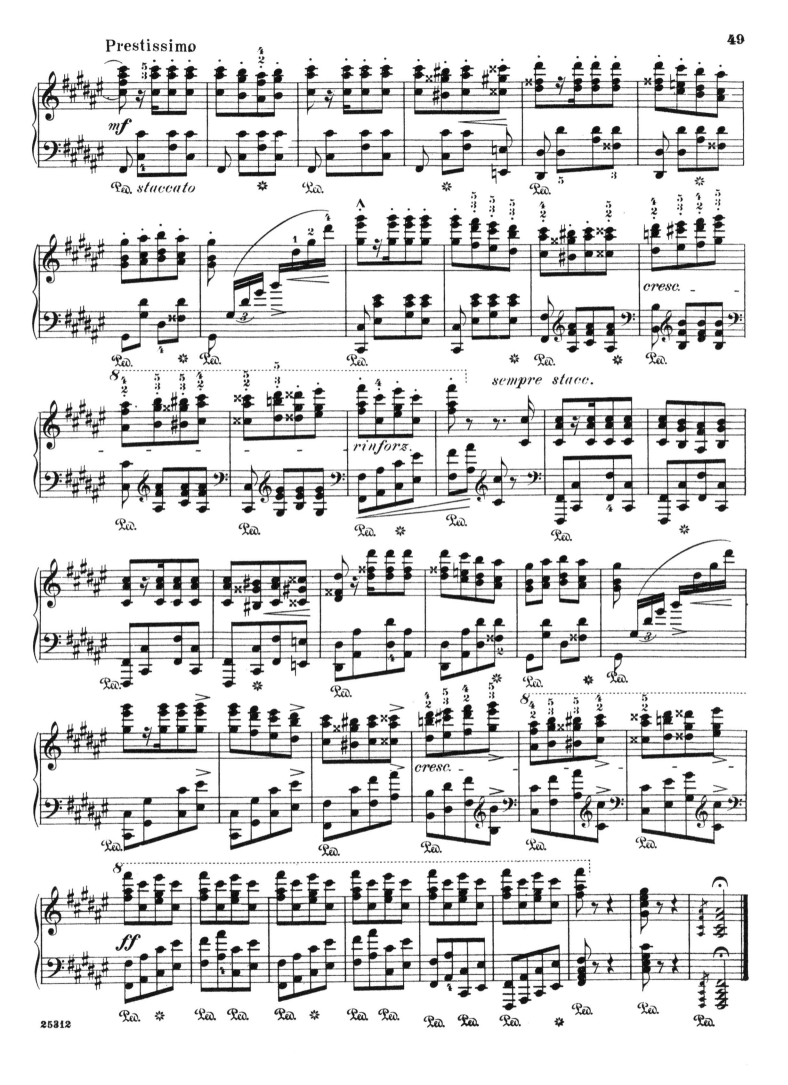

A.J. Joachim

Rhapsodie hongroise No. 12

**Edited and fingered by
Rafael Joseffy**

Franz Liszt

Introduzione
Mesto

Piano

* Take notes with up-stems with the right hand: those having down-stems, with the left hand

25312   Printed in the U. S. A.

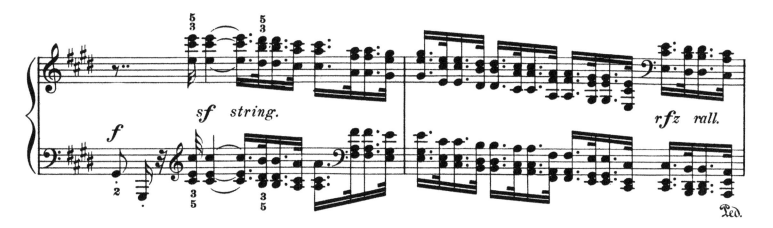

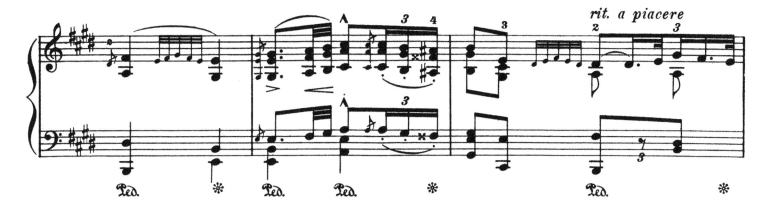

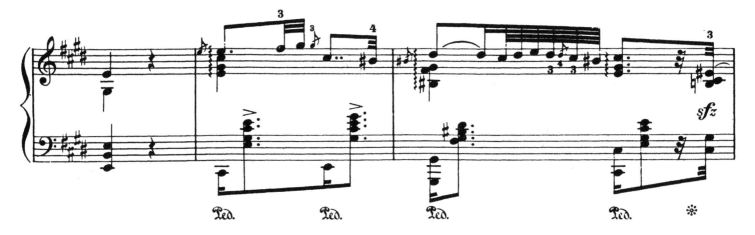

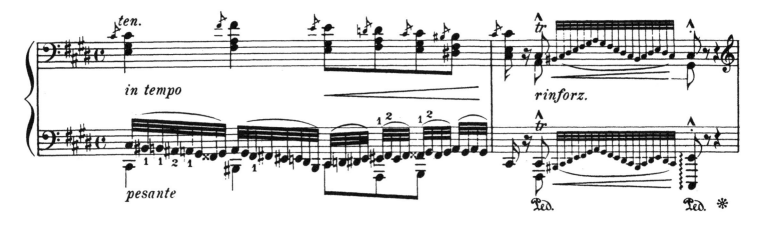

Allegro zingarese

sempre dolce ma ben marcata la melodia

rit. *in tempo* *con due Pedali*

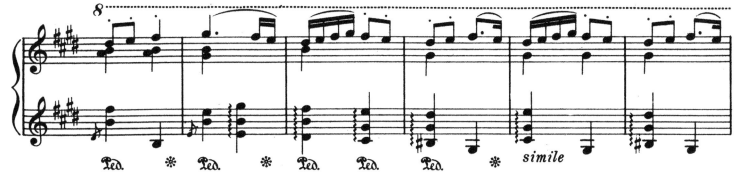

simile

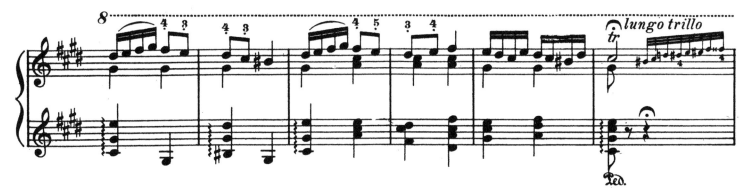

lungo trillo

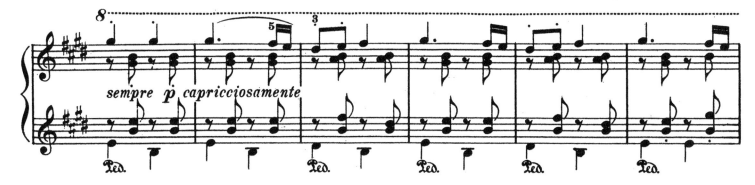

sempre p capricciosamente

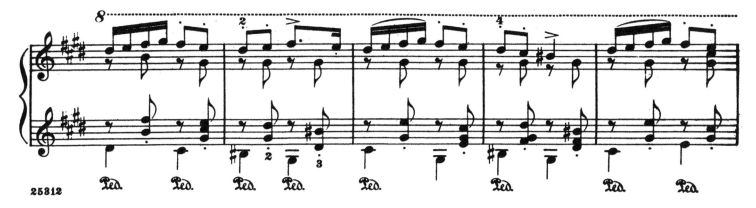

un poco accel.   dim.

Un poco più vivo

sempre *p* quasi campanelle
non legato

simile

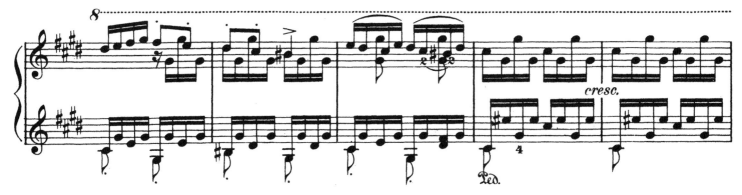

cresc.

dim.   smorz.   **ppp**

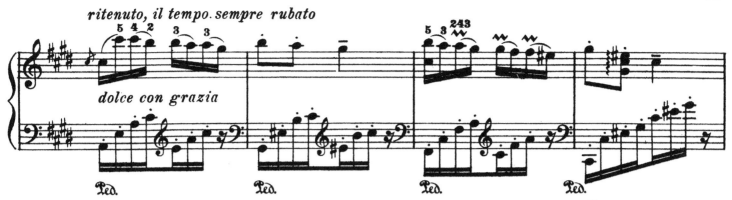

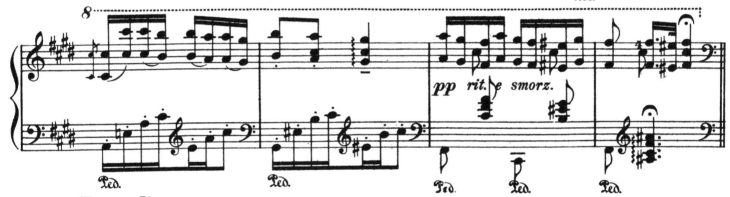

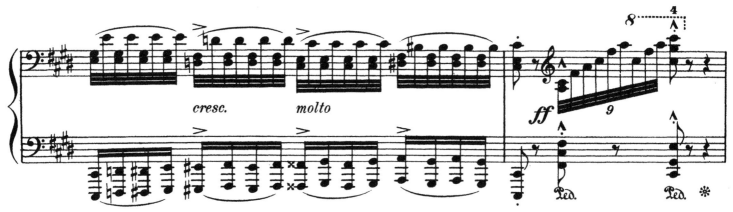

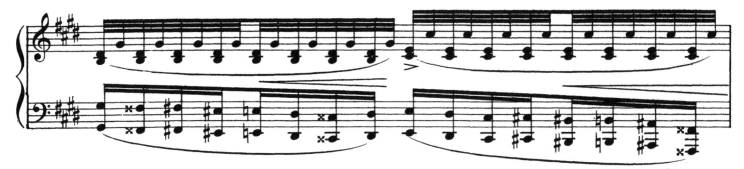

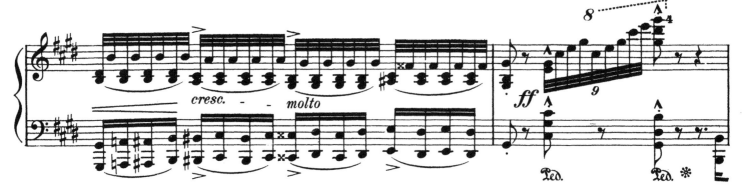

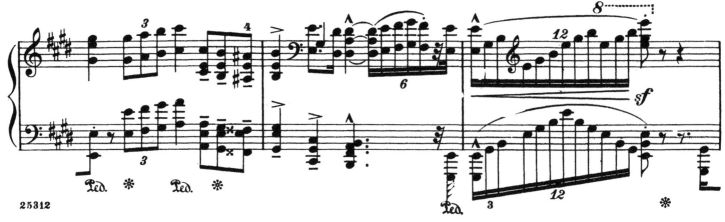

Allegretto giojoso

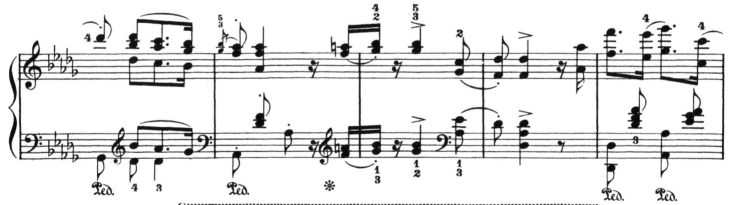

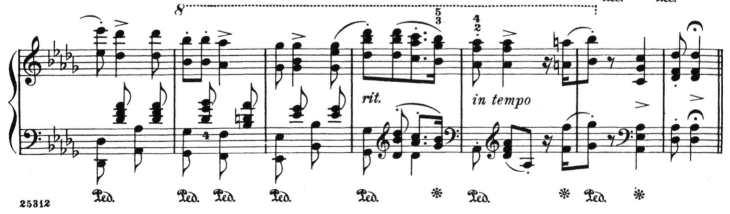

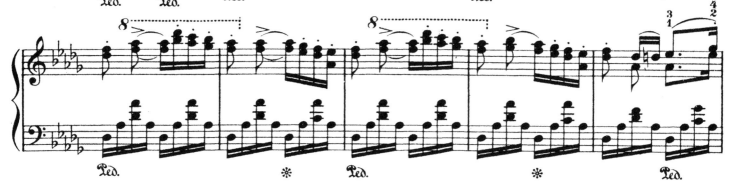

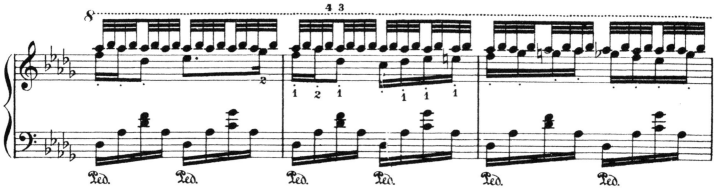

25312

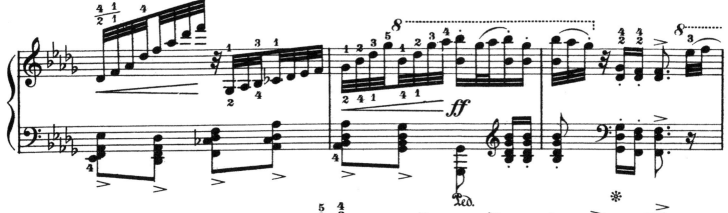

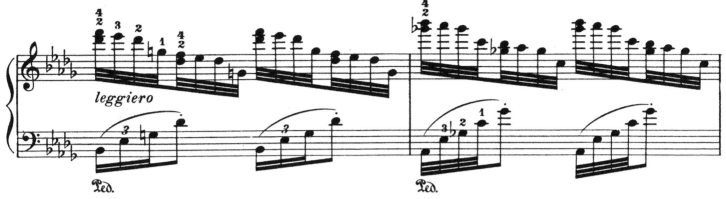

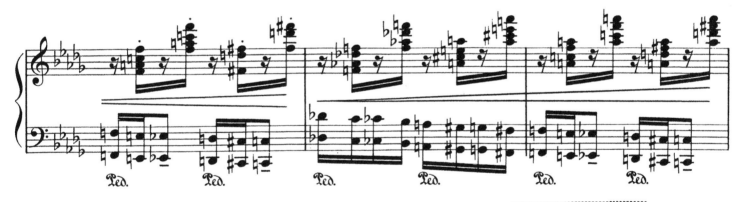

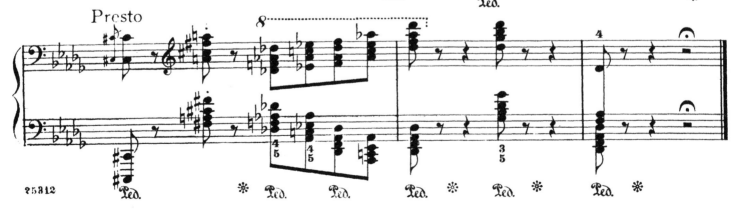

Au Comte Léo Festetics

Rhapsodie hongroise № 13

Edited and fingered by
Rafael Joseffy

FRANZ LISZT

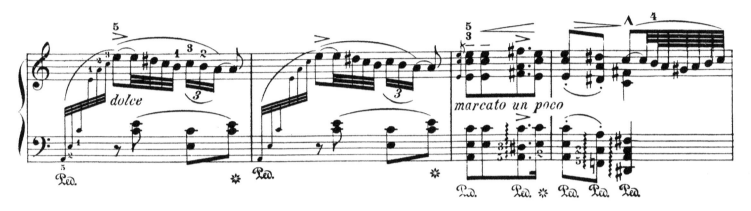

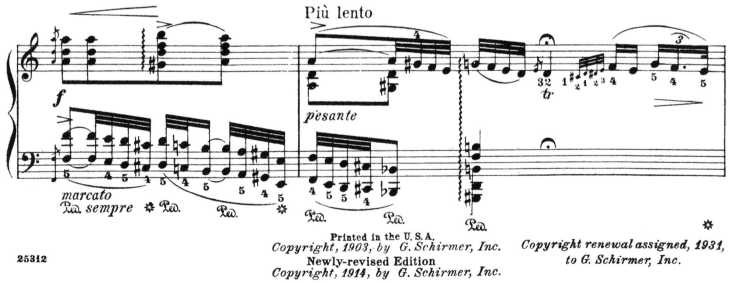

25312

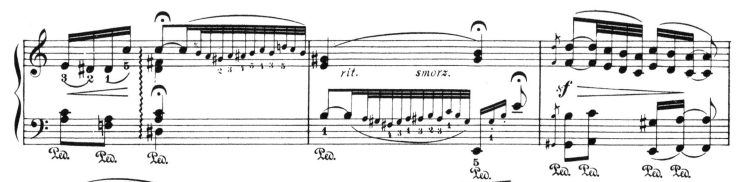

Più lento

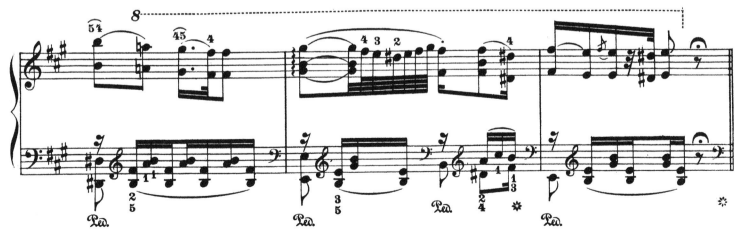

25812

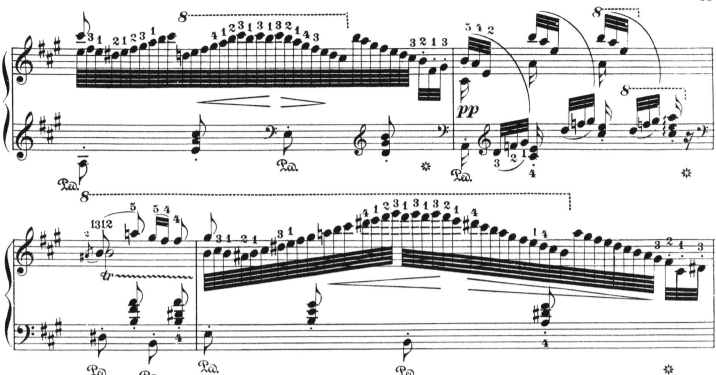

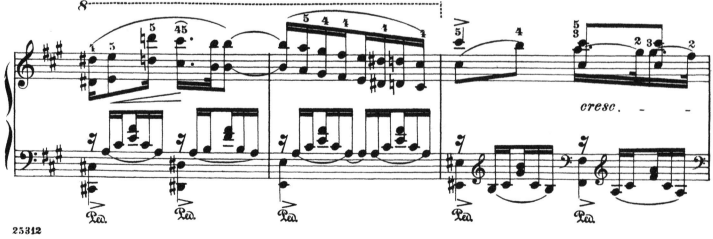

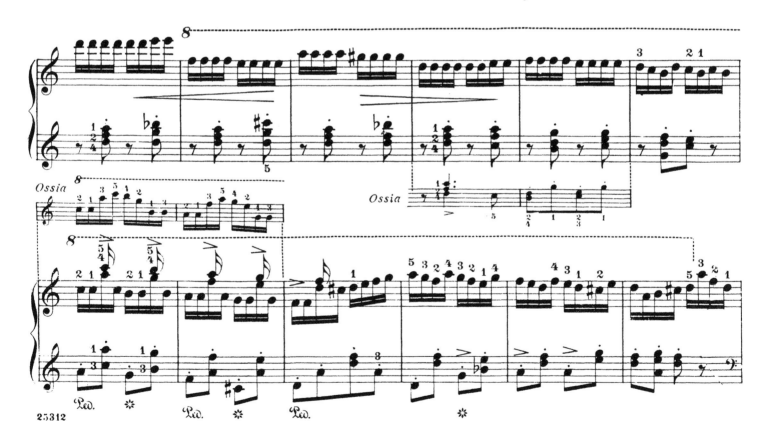

simile

sempre p e leggiero

Ossia

Ossia

Ossia

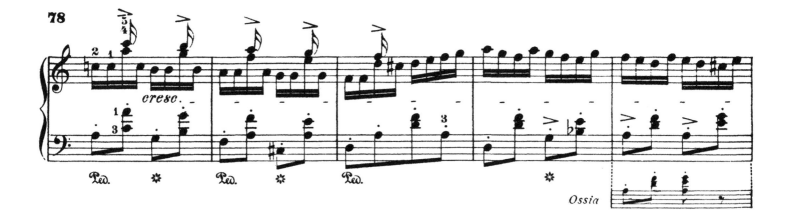

Presto assai

à Hans G. von Bülow

Rhapsodie hongroise № 14

Edited and fingered by
Rafael Joseffy

FRANZ LISZT

Lento quasi Marcia funèbre

Piano

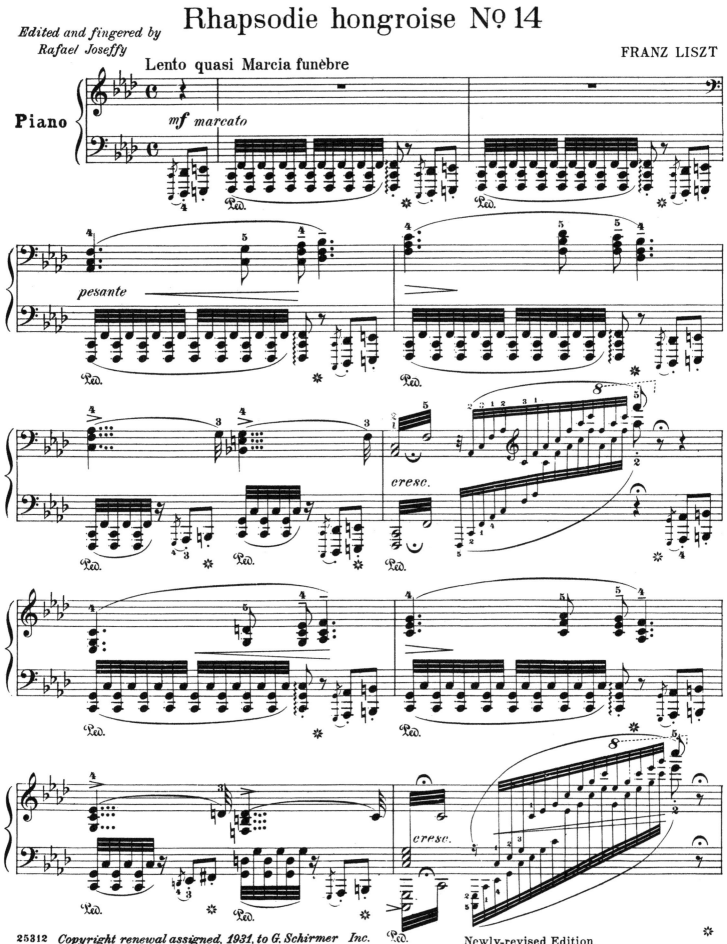

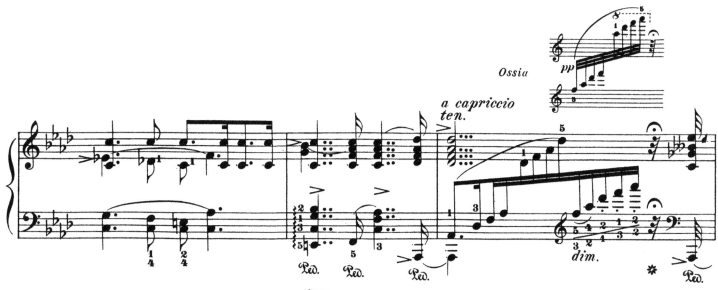

25312

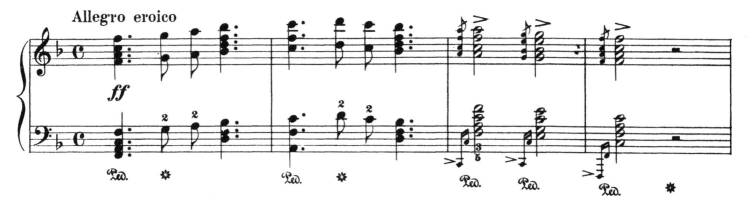

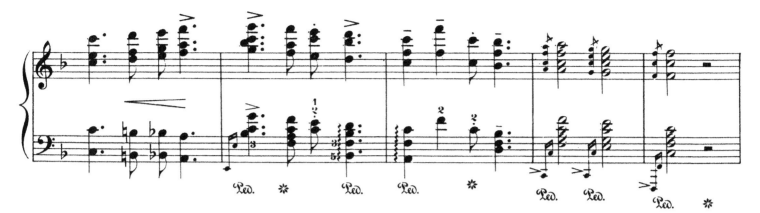

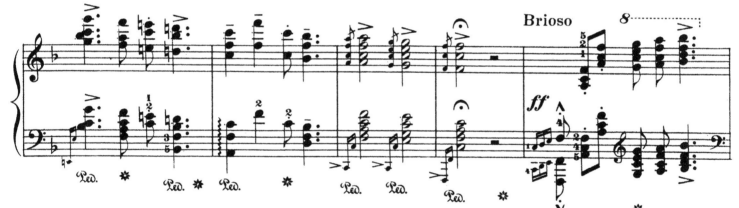

Brioso

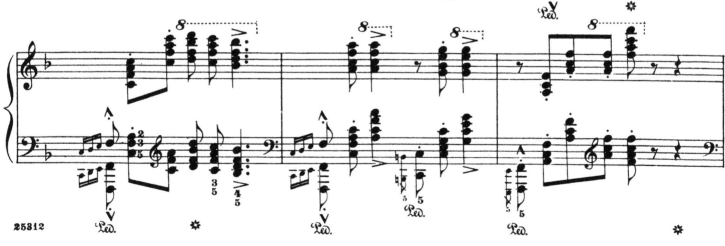

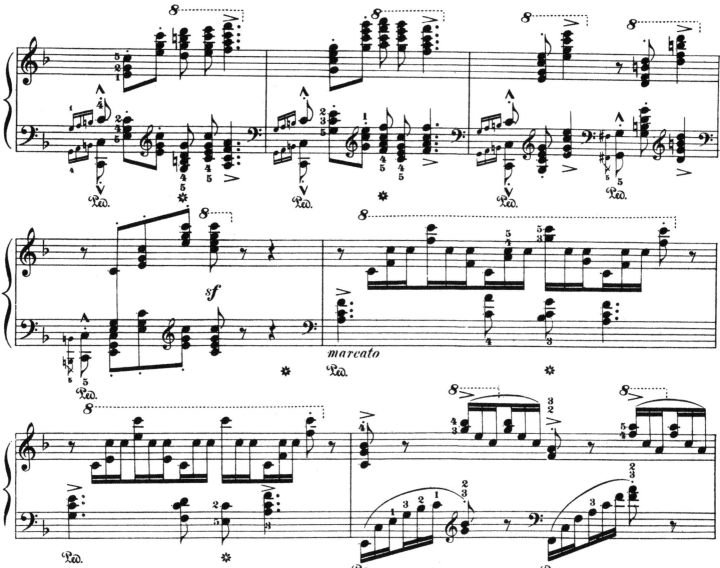

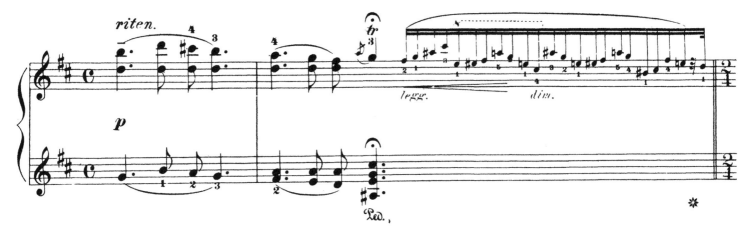

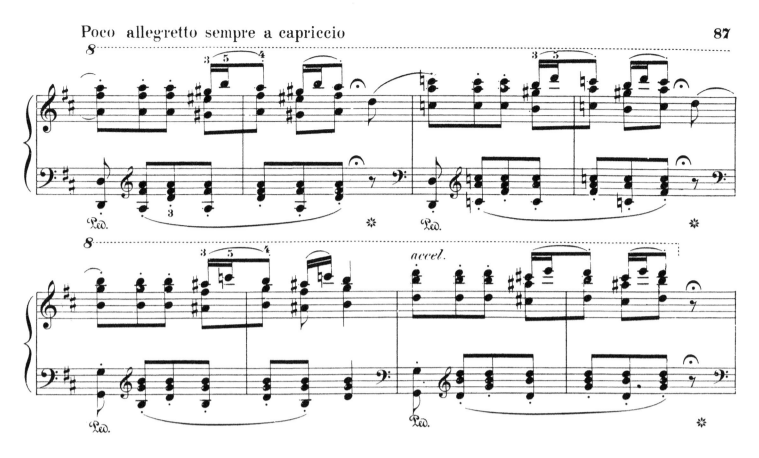

Allegretto alla Zingarese

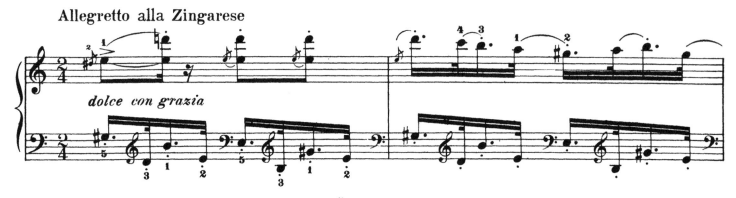

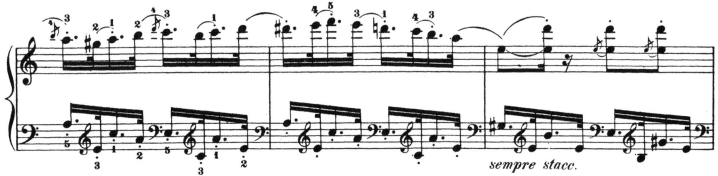

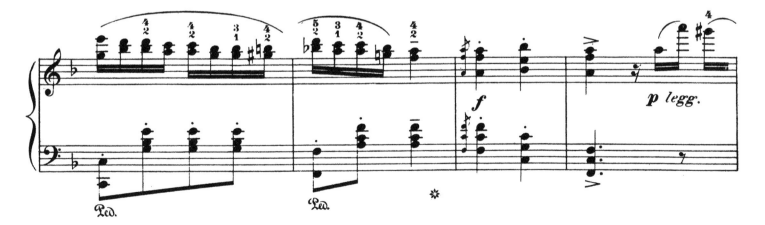

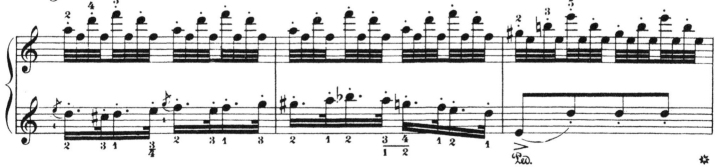

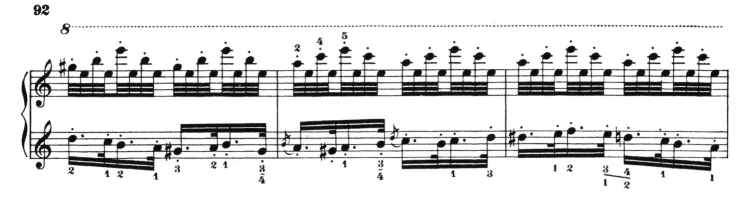

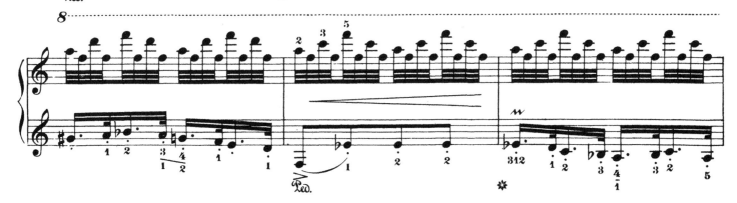

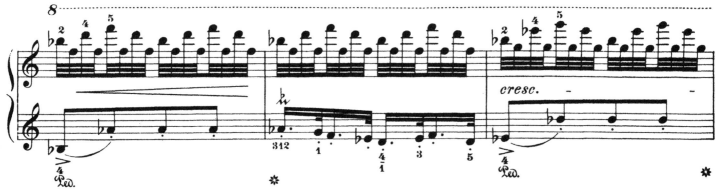

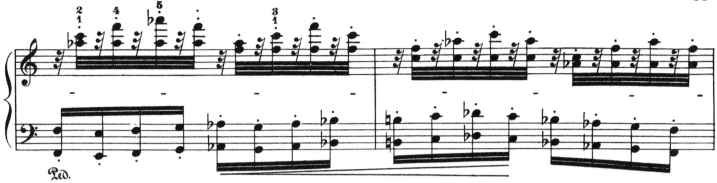

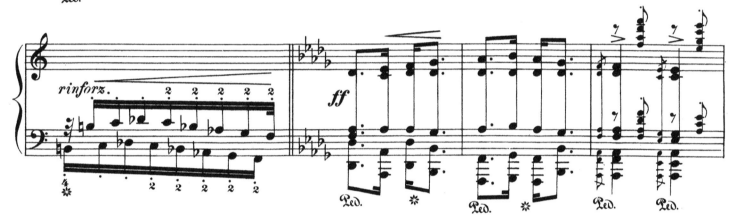

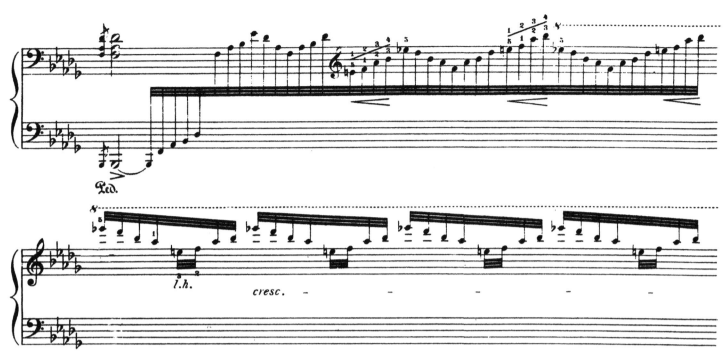

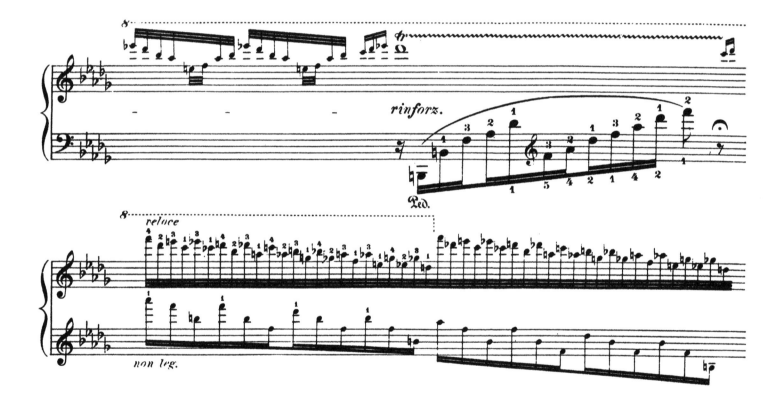

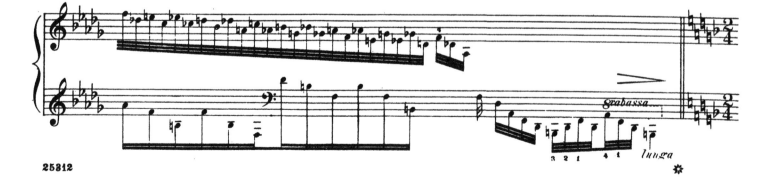

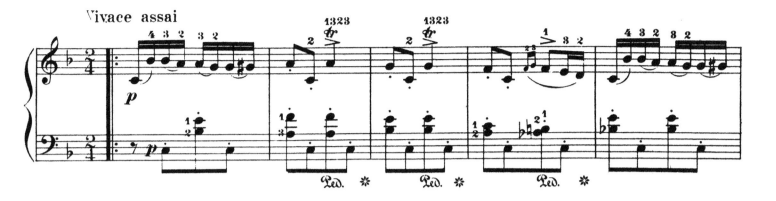

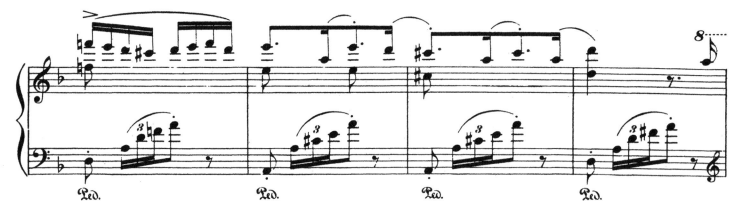

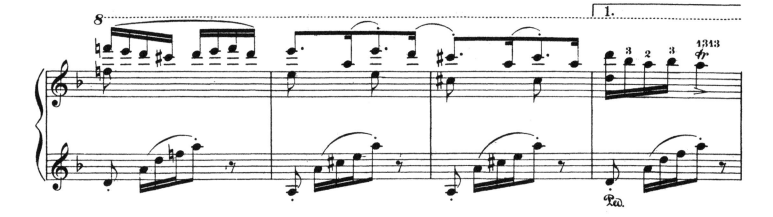

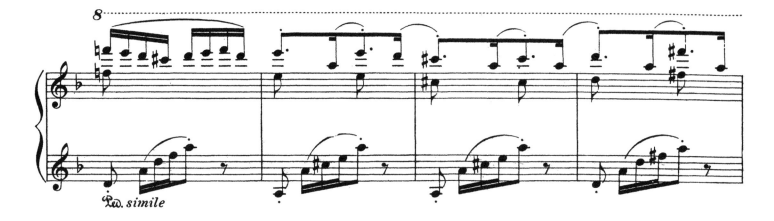

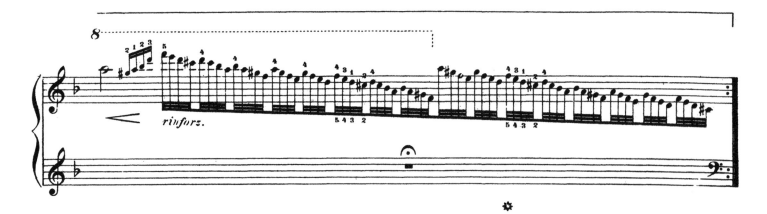

ff *sfogato con bravura*

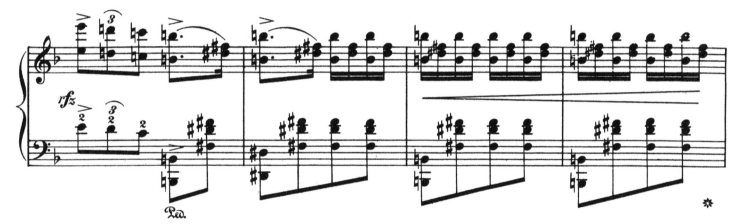

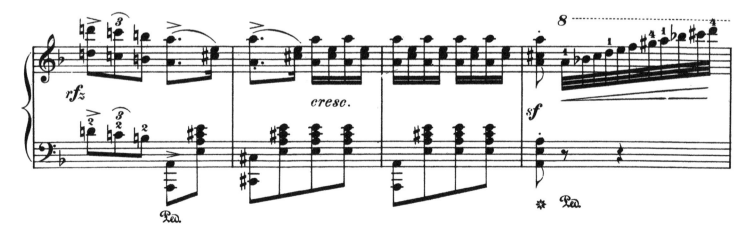

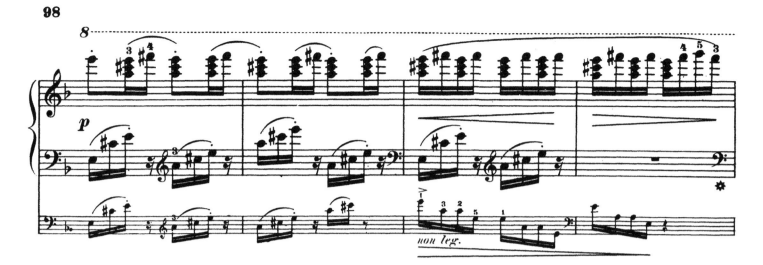

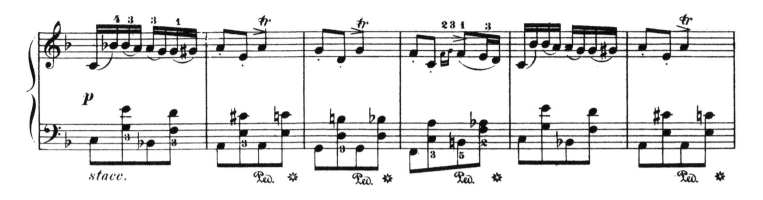

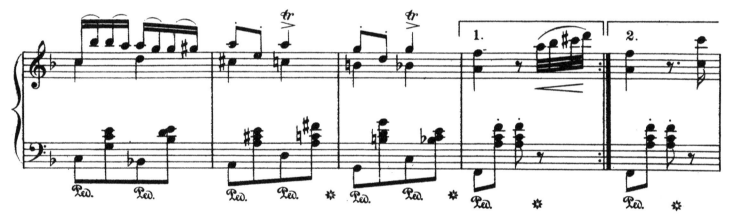

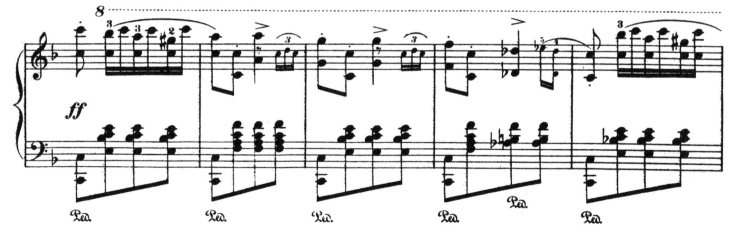

Più allegro

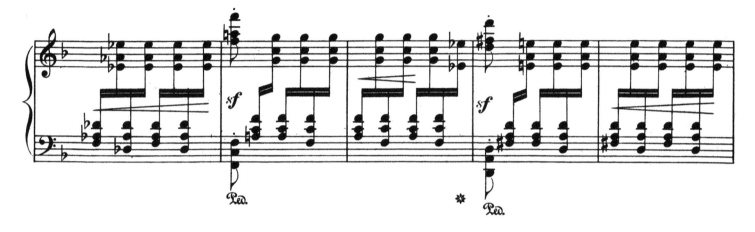

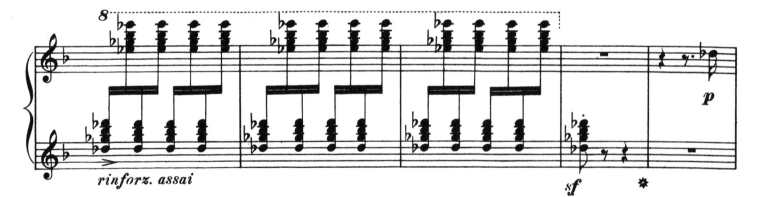

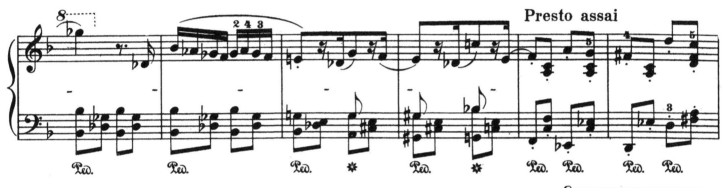

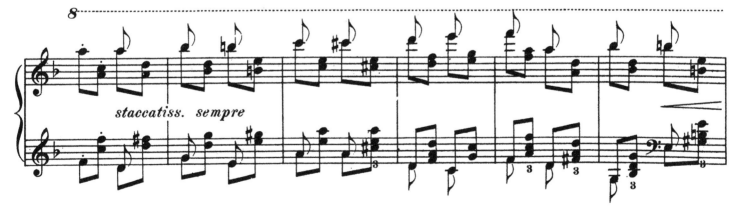

Allegro brioso

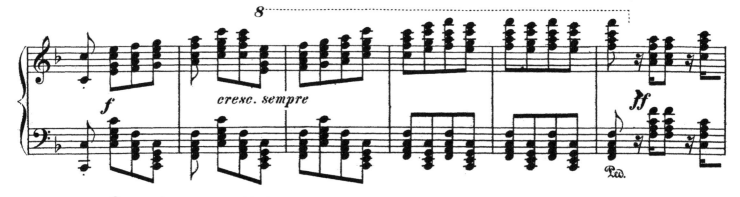

Rhapsodie hongroise № 15

Rákóczy March

Edited and fingered by
Rafael Joseffy

Arranged by
Franz Liszt

Printed in the U. S. A.
Copyright, 1902, by G. Schirmer, Inc.
Newly-revised Edition
Copyright, 1914, by G. Schirmer, Inc.

strepitoso molto rinforz.
8
ff
Tempo di marcia animato
marcatissimo
Ped.
sempre ff
8
Ped.
8
Ped.

25312

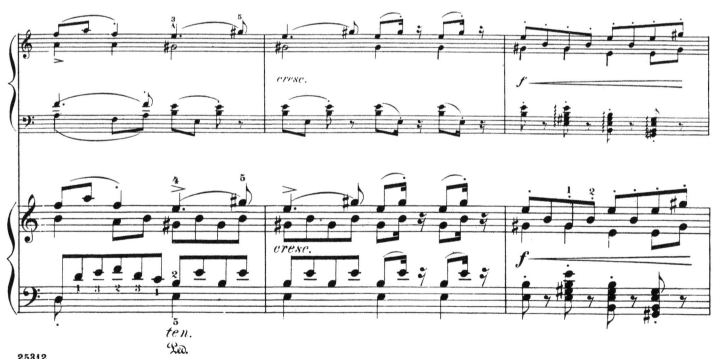

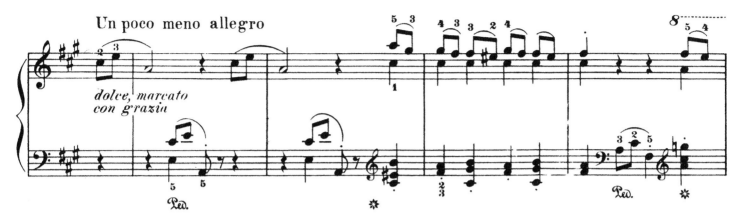

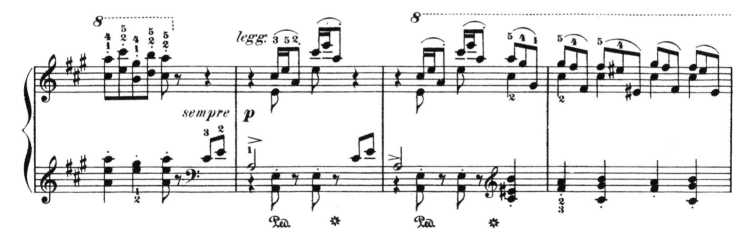

25312

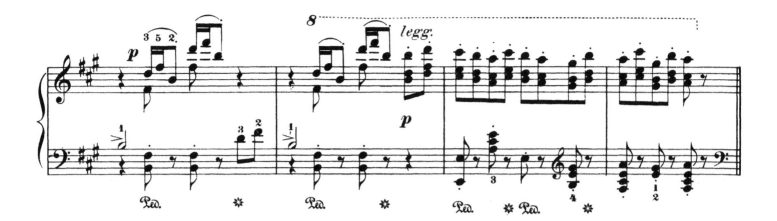

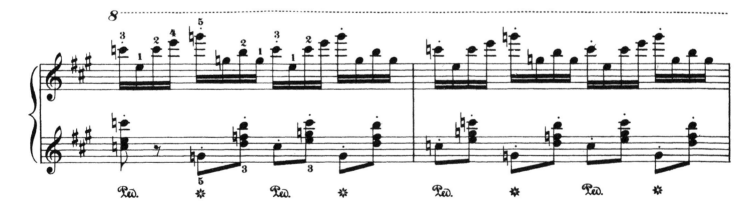

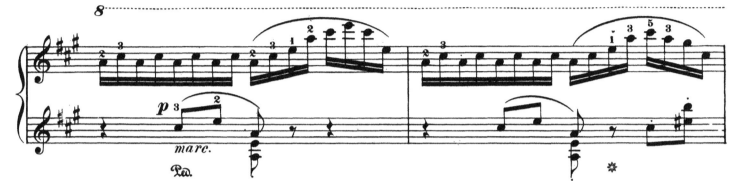

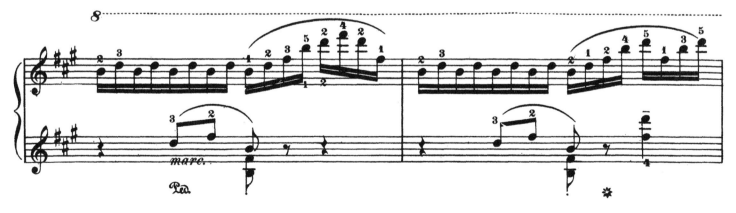

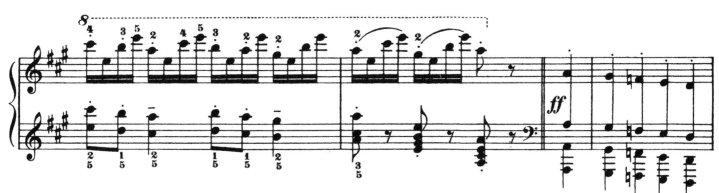

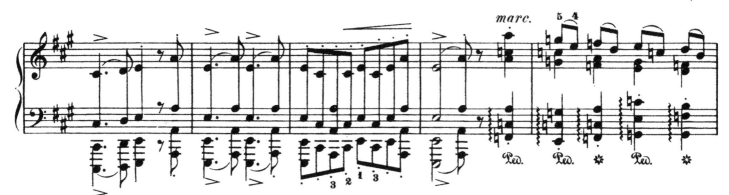

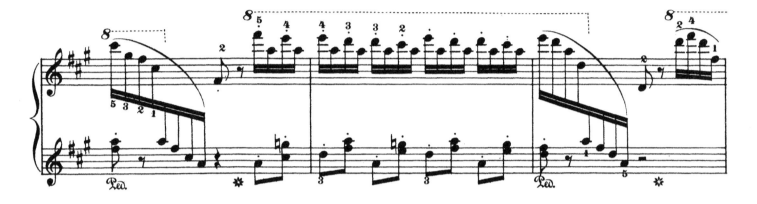

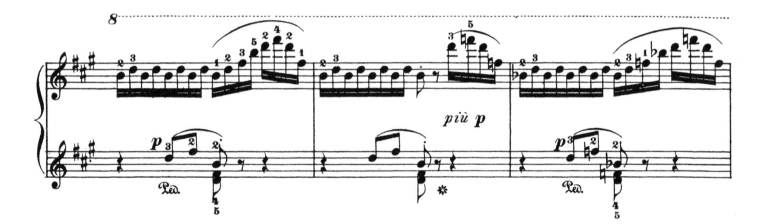

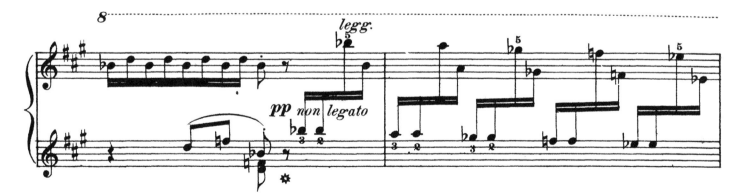

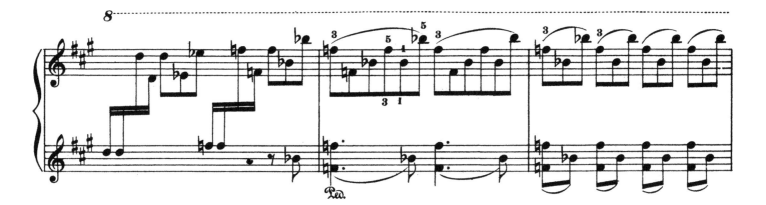

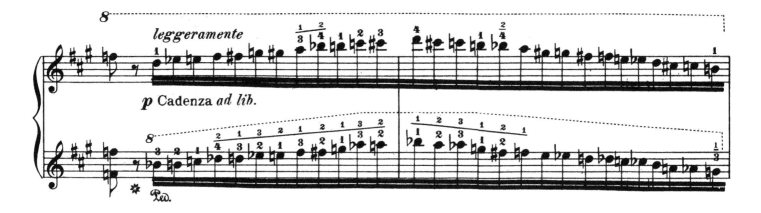

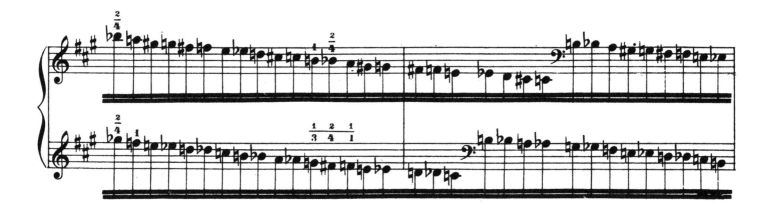

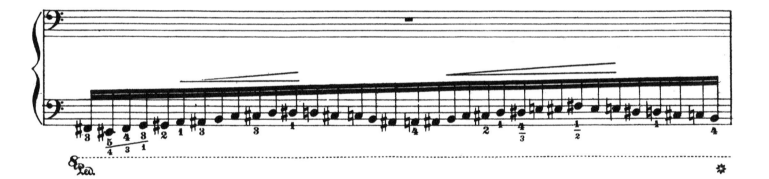

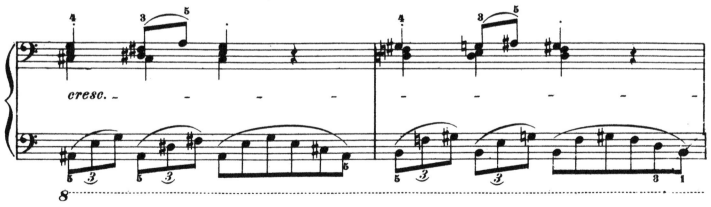

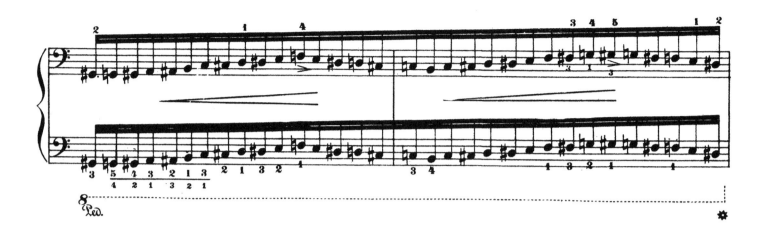

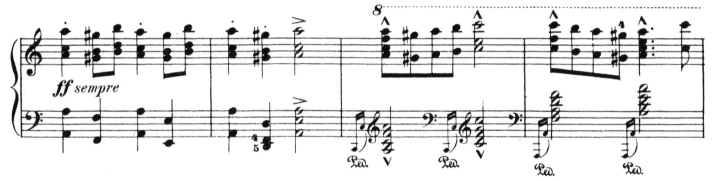

25312

Facilité

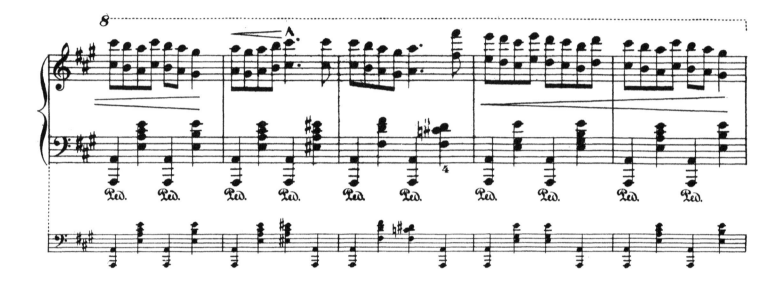

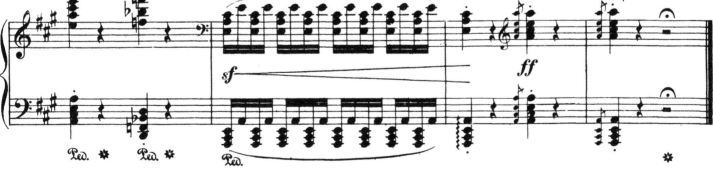